A PECULIAR YOUNG MAN

A Peculiar Young Man

WILL WILLIS III

PALMETTO
PUBLISHING
Charleston, SC
www.PalmettoPublishing.com

Copyright © 2024 by Will Willis III

All rights reserved

No portion of this book may be reproduced, stored in a retrieval system, or transmitted in any form by any means–electronic, mechanical, photocopy, recording, or other–except for brief quotations in printed reviews, without prior permission of the author.

Paperback ISBN: 979-8-8229-5419-9
eBook ISBN: 979-8-8229-3612-6

CONTENTS

Acknowledgements	vii
Foreword	ix
Introduction	xi
Chapter 1: The Beginning	1
Chapter 2: Education	7
Chapter 3: Relationship/Admiration	13
Chapter 4: Ministry/Music	21
Chapter 5: Godsons	28
Chapter 6: Overcoming Flaws	50
Chapter 8: Epilogue	56
Psalm	57
Goals; Prayers; Revelations; Proverbs and Sayings; Fun Facts	59
Musical Piece	67
Business Information	69

Acknowledgements

First, I want to give honor to my God, who is the head of my life, my Savior, and my Lord, Jesus Christ. If it were not for Him, I do not know where I would be today. I want to thank my siblings, Gabrielle Willis, Emanuell Willis, and Michall Willis for being the best siblings I could ever have. I want to thank my godsons, Tyrick Nelson and Tyrone McGhee. I want to thank my godparents, Joseph Casby Sr., John Gordon IV, Samuel Green Jr., Shalonda Spencer, PhD, Tayisha Green, and the Late Carolyn Spencer for their love and support. I want to give special thanks to my parents, Will and Nellie Willis for raising me the right way spiritually and naturally. I am proud to be their son. I am the man I am today because of them. Also, a special thanks to my grandmothers, Viola T. Spencer and late Annette Jones-Bickham for putting holiness inside my parents and especially to my great-grandmother, Overseer, Apostle Mary J. Trask. I want to give my dad, Will Willis Jr. extra special Thanks for helping me write this book. If it were not for him, I do not think I would have been able to finish it. I want to also give a special thanks to my lovely auntie, who I call Teedy, Angela L. Spencer-Green, MEd, my cousin, Lathaniel C. Green Jr., and Laya Jack-Simmons, MA, for editing this book. I could not do it without them. I want to thank the cover designer, Jason LeBlanc. I want to thank all my grandparents, aunts, uncles, cousins, and church family (House of Deliverance Church, Inc.).

Foreword

Will Willis III is a son, a brother, a godfather, a leader, a teacher, and a mentor, but most of all, he is a Man of God. We should know because we are his Parents. Lil Will loves pleasing and doing the will of GOD. Most young boys loved playing games and playing jokes on others, but his desire was always to be a leader, to help others, and to be dutiful in church. Growing up, he used to say, "I am going to be like Martin Luther King Jr." He may or may not one day be as famous as MLK, but we know he is on his way to being as great because one's greatness is determined by the positive impact you have in others' lives. We believe all will enjoy this book. Give every young person this book and let Lil Will encourage them through his life. Every young person needs to be encouraged about living for GOD, not let difficult situations define them, or stop who they can become in Life, and Most of All in CHRIST.

We Love You Son

Introduction

This book is about a young man who wants to show that everyone is not the same. Many people stereotype young African American males, P.K.s, Christians, and black Christian musicians. They have been given a bad name. However, this book will show that there is someone who is after God's own heart.

You will read about the life of a young man from birth to young adulthood, who, while growing up, realized how firstborn males in the Bible were special in God's eyes, but because of disobedience, jealousy, and pride they did not always receive God's blessing. This tragic misfortune occurred more than once in the Bible, but the young man in this book was determined not to share their story. You will read about his shortcomings and how he overcame them to become the great man of God that he is today. So, enjoy this glimpse into the life of Lil Will III.

CHAPTER 1

The Beginning

In New Orleans, Louisiana on September 2, 1994, at about 2:30 a.m., before birth, the baby swallowed bile in the amniotic fluid. After birth, their son was immediately rushed to the neonatal ICU where doctors performed many tests and procedures. The doctor informed the young couple that the baby's condition was called meconium, which builds up inside the intestines by swallowing amniotic fluid. As a result, there are one out of three things could happen. The baby could pull through and be fine, mentally challenged, or he could die.

For three weeks the baby boy was in an incubator with needles and tubes hooked to his little body. He was under twenty-four-hour supervision by the doctors and nurses and twenty-four-hour prayer by the saints of God. When he took a breath, it was a horrifying sight. The condition affected his lungs and their ability to adequately inflate, which caused his stomach and chest to cave in deeply because it was so hard for him to breathe. Every breath seemed to be his last and it did not seem he would recover at all. However, things began to change quickly because his family were praying and fasting for a miracle. His color and breathing began to normalize. The oxygen and feeding tubes were soon removed from his little body. Three weeks later, the doctor finally released him. He said those words that every loving parent wants to hear, "Mr. and Mrs. Willis you have a healthy baby boy." This marked the beginning of a remarkable life's journey for Will Willis III.

Lil Will, as he was affectionately called, grew strong in the Lord because his father rededicated his life to God and taught his son all about God. Will Jr., while sitting in the balcony of their second-floor apartment many days and nights in New Orleans east, would sit his son on his knee and tell him stories. They were not fairytales, but true stories of great men and women of God from the Bible. After each story he always told Lil Will that someday he would be a great man of God just like Moses and David.

Will Jr. played sports (tracks, football, etc.) growing up for the neighborhood park and in high school. He had the opportunity to play college ball. Will Jr.'s mom asked him not to go away, so he stayed. He had many trophies, medals, ribbons, and two letterman jackets. But with all that, Lil Will did not know anything about his father's athletic background until about the age of nine. When Lil Will was born and his father returned to God, Will Jr. put all his awards away. He told his wife that he did not want his children to see his accomplishments in worldly activities because they could be a distraction. Will Jr. vowed to the Lord that he would raise an army for Him, and it started with Lil Will. His parents bought him musical instruments to bang on as they sang gospel songs and played church at home. Church was and still is a great part of his life. Most kids' first words are "momma" and "dada", but Will's first words were "Oh, Oh Jesus," which he picked up from a song by Bishop Paul S. Morton Sr. and the Greater St. Stephen Mass Choir called "Who's the One." He listened to that song so many times that his first words were, "Oh, Oh Jesus." His parents were so excited that they called everyone so that they could hear him say, "Oh, Oh Jesus." That

Sunday at Church the minister of music and church choir sang the song for him. He stood up in front of the church in the aisle with his plastic microphone singing with them. Will Jr. told Nellie, "That's what happens when you put a mic in your baby's hands instead of a football."

As God began to bless him as a toddler, the enemy tried to step in and derail his future. His Maw-Maw, his parental grandmother, noticed that he kept to himself and that he did not always respond to their first call. Sometimes they had to get his attention before he responded. His doctor informed his parents he would grow out of it, and some babies take longer than others to develop. His Maw-Maw did not receive that and continued to pray. She urged his parents to change his doctors or get a second opinion. Will Jr. told a co-worker what was going on, and his co-worker said his children's pediatrician made house calls when they were not able to get them to the hospital. The co-worker informed Will Jr. that Dr. C. Turner also worked with Children's Hospital. Lil Will's parents said they knew after the first visit Dr. Turner was the pediatrician for him. In the past, when Lil Will was a baby and a toddler, he fought the doctors. He kicked, punched, and screamed at the doctors, but not Dr.

Turner. Lil Will's parents said he was nervous, but not frightened. Dr. Turner became the Willis' pediatrician. She confirmed what his Maw-Maw had told his parents – there was something going on with his ears. She referred his parents to Dr. M. Hagmann, an ear, nose, and throat doctor at Children's Hospital. Lil Will did not trust him right away. His parents said-he did not want doctor to touch him. At the first visit, when he tried to check Lil Will's throat with the tongue depressor, he bit it in half. Dr. Hagmann said it was the first time that had ever happened. He asked what had happened to him to make him so aggressive. As time went by, he and Lil Will became buddies.

Dr. Hagmann diagnosed Lil Will with a Chronic Middle Ear Infection or Otitis Media (O.M.), which filled his ear with fluid when his middle ear was infected.

He suggested a simple procedure called Tympanostomy Tube Surgery, which tubes would be inserted into his ears to drain the fluid. His parents noticed the doctor looked concerned, and they asked him if there was something else. Dr. Hagmann went on to tell them of the late diagnosis, Lil Will could have delays in speech development and learning. However, he performed the surgery, and all went well.

Lil Will's Maw-Maw said she could remember the first time he was able to hear clearly. She and Angela, his Teedy, were in the car talking normally, and he began to repeat what they were saying. She excitedly told his aunt, "He could hear!" She whispered the alphabets to him, and he repeated them back to her and she began to cry. Soon after, Lil Will began his speech development classes.

CHAPTER 2

Education

Lil Will's first experience with education was at Bolden Childcare. It was not a pleasant experience for him because it was his first time being away from his parents. Between the hours of 8 am to 5 pm he fought and cried. Three weeks after enrolling him in BCC, Nellie found out that she was expecting another baby. The doctor asked her to stop working because she was having complications. Nellie took Lil Will out of daycare and taught him at home. She noticed Lil Will enjoyed watching Sesame Street and how quickly he learned his letters and numbers. Lil Will's parents invested in the Hooked-on-Phonics program, which he really enjoyed.

At the age of five, Lil Will attended St. Simon Peter, elementary Catholic school. It was like déjà vu to the parents. He cried and did not want them to leave him, but they knew he was in good hands. His teacher, Ms. Batiste, was an angel. She told them, "I got it…you can go ahead." Lil Will's parents were nervous the whole day and looked forward to 3 pm to see how Lil Will made out. Ms. Batiste informed the parents that Lil Will did fine. As weeks went by, Ms. Batiste noticed that Lil Will did not talk as much; he was shy and did not interact with classmates sometimes because of his speech. Due to his hearing delay, Lil Will developed a speech impediment. Ms. Batiste informed his parents that he should be enrolled in the Title I program at St. Simon Peter. She told them it would not interfere with his class work or cause him to fall behind, but it would help him with his speech and forming sentences. Lil Will did not let his speech impediment slow him down. He excelled in Title I and schoolwork.

Will stayed at St. Simon Peter until second grade because his great-grandmother had a vision of opening a school for children to be in a Christian and safe environment. The students did not only learn academics, but they learned the ways of God. The name of the school was Beginning Visions Progressive Academy (BVPA). Beginning Visions used the Accelerated Christian Education (ACE) curriculum. The ACE program was a Bible-based, K-12 program for students to learn individually at their own pace. Lil Will was at BVPA for twelve years but later attended Louisiana High School to receive his high school diploma equivalency. Lil Will's best years were at Beginning Visions where he received countless awards and made numerous accomplishments. When he was in third grade, he received the Christian Character Award; he won Prom King four times in a row, was in SGA four years consecutively and was elected president twice. He also won multiple medals by competing in the ACE Regional Student Convention where other schools using the ACE curriculum came together and competed in different events. He helped his school win a first and third place overall plaque in platform and music at the ACE Regional Student Convention. He also helped his school win the Christian Character Award, which was like a million bucks to him. He had the honor of going with his school to the ACE International Student Convention where they competed against all schools from around the world. Lil Will got to march and hold the banner for their region because his school had won Christian Character Award.

At BVPA, he received the Spirit Award every year until he left and was on the honor roll until High

School, but midway through his freshman year, he began to slack up on his schoolwork and homework, which was the beginning of him falling behind. After a couple of years, steadily backsliding in his schoolwork, Lil Will and his father had a heart-to-heart talk. Lil Will's Father and one of his younger siblings had previously talked about getting their G.E.D, but Lil Will's desire was to graduate from Beginning Visions. Lil Will's father told him, "You may not want to give up, but in your heart, you have already given up." Lil Will was discouraged and disappointed in himself because he allowed himself to fall behind and waited too late to correct the problem. Another reason, he felt funny about his younger siblings finishing school and attending college at the same time with him when he was supposed to be their example. It just did not seem right to him that a twenty-year-old, a seventeen-year-old, a sixteen-year-old, and a fifteen-year-old were finishing school together. He had reminded himself what his grandmother told him, that it was not about age, but it was about finishing. Lil Will and his younger siblings decided to go to G.E.D. school and take their journey together.

Lil Will had gone to Louisiana High School in March 2015 and finished in three months. He and siblings had finished around the same time. Lil Will went straight to Delgado Community College, but he was very indecisive about his Major. He had gone from Veterinary Tech to Child Development for Young Children to Business and Management with a concentration in Music Business and a Certificate of Entrepreneurship. He was still ashamed because his siblings were in college with him, but he always heard people say it was so cool. Lil Will finally realized they were each other's strength. When Lil Will went to Delgado, he was not trying to be in any programs, organizations, or clubs. He was just trying to focus on finishing school. Therefore, he found himself in many programs. He started doing work study, became a SGA senator, and he became a part of TRiO/Student Support Services, a federally funded program that helps students to graduate with a degree. He joined the National Society of Leadership and Success, and he also was a member of Alpha Beta Gamma, an international business honor society and Start Up U, which helped scholars who want to become entrepreneurs and start their businesses to grow their network. Lil Will was trying to do it all. He had school, ministry, godsons, family, mentoring and helping others. Academic Advisors told him that he had too much on his plate. He soon realized he had to slow down and that is exactly what he did. He set his priorities, and he began to see the difference in his schoolwork. One semester he made the honor roll and the Dean's list. He was awarded two scholarships, one from Delgado and one from the New Orleans Delta Foundation Scholarship. TRiO hosted their own ceremony for students who were part of their program, and he was honored. Every ceremony TRiO honored one student with the Jefferey Washington Leadership Award. Lil Will received that award along with the award for outstanding leadership and his commitment to the Student Support Services at Delgado. Lil Will graduated with an Associate Degree in Business and Management with a concentration in Music Business and a certification of Entrepreneurship from Delgado Community College. Lil Will continued his education at the University of New Orleans and graduated with a bachelor's degree in Management with a concentration in Human Resource Management.

CHAPTER 3

Relationship/Admiration

Lil Will's parents had three more children. The second-born was a little girl named Gabrielle, whom they called Gabby. Gabby was girly and stand-offish. Her parents treated her like a baby doll. Growing up, Lil Will was close to Gabby because of her maturity. A year after Gabby's birth, their parents had a boy named Emanuell. They called him Manny because he acted like a little man. Manny was playful and very talkative. There were times they would look for Manny and he would be outside or around the corner the sharing gospel of Jesus Christ with a child or an adult in the neighborhood. Manny was Lil Will's roommate and play buddy. They were also spiritually close. They enjoyed talking about the Word of God and listening to and talking about Gospel music. A year later, Lil Will's parents had another little girl named Michall. They called her Kelly. Kelly was Gabby's roommate, and they enjoyed playing dress up and playing with their baby dolls. But there were times when Kelly enjoyed playing superheroes and having wrestling matches with her older brother, something her older sister would never do. Will Jr and Nellie wanted everyone in their household to have names that were spiritually meaningful, that included having double L's. You will also notice the two sisters were named after two angels, Gabriel and Michael.

Before moving on, you should know that they are all miracles. When Nellie was thirteen, she was diagnosed with kidney failure. The doctors wanted to place her on a kidney machine. Doctors said without the kidney machine she would never live to see 21. She was also told there was a good chance she would not have any children. With tears rolling down her face, she told her mother she did not want to be hooked to a machine. Her mother looked into her eyes and said, "You have to believe that God can heal you." Her mother continued and told her that there was a Healing Revival in town and they would go that night. Nellie sat in church taking in every word of the Evangelist, waiting patiently for the woman of God to call for a prayer line. The Holy Spirit moved upon the church and worship began. At that time, the Evangelist, Mary Trask, called for a prayer line. Nellie quickly walked up; she was first in line. She and her mother began to pray and ask God for a healing. She began to tell the woman of God what the doctors said. The Evangelist asked her if she believed that God could heal her kidneys and she said, "Yes!" She anointed Nellie with blessed oil and laid her hand upon her head. She began to pray for her and told her that God was doing a spiritual operation on her, and He was giving her two new kidneys. Nellie felt something come over her body, and she fell out. When she arose to go back to her seat, the woman of God said, "Wait, baby, how do you feel?" Lil Will's mother yelled, "I am healed…I felt Him go through my body!" The woman of God laid her hands on her again, and Nellie began to dance and praise the Lord. The Evangelist told her that when she went back to see the doctors, they were going to be amazed because she was healed. The Evangelist also told her to tell them God had healed her. Many years later, Nellie married the Evangelist's grandson, Will Jr.

Now, as parents, Will and Nellie were very protective because they knew that their children were miracles, special gifts from God. Lil Will's parents invested a lot of spiritual time, money, and love into the children's lives. In their early years, their parents were very particular about who they spent time with. They were not able to spend the night away from home, and they were not able to go to a lot of "fun" places because of the worldly surroundings. They really believe evil communications corrupt good manners, so they sheltered their children as much as they could. Many people admired how their parents raised them in Christ. Their parents believed their surroundings would influence their behavior. They were taught that respect was very important in a family. It was okay to have disagreements, but to argue, to fight, and to disrespect one another was not allowed. Lil Will and his siblings were not allowed to disagree because their dad believed it was arguing, and he wanted to make sure that they did not go to the extreme or get too serious. Through the years, Lil Will recalls, although there were disagreements, they never fought, disrespected, or called each other derogatory names. As the siblings got older, they became closer. They did everything and went just about everywhere with each other. When other siblings or young adults saw how close they were, they were surprised because they did not have that same relationship with their families. The young people were surprised about how much they (parents and children) collectively did with each other. They told Lil Will and his siblings, "We did not have that same relationship with our families." Lil Will and his siblings were surprised to hear that because they thought all homes had that same type of relationship. Their father, Will Jr., taught them, "At the end of the day, when everything is over, you will just have each other. So, watch each other's backs." Will Jr. was a family man. He is similar to a few well-known American TV dads such as Cliff Huxtable, Philip Banks, Carl Winslow, and Charles Ingalls. Will Jr. told his children, "Whatever you do, you have to make sure you make wise decisions and choices. You represent your family, your grandmother, your great-grandmother, your church, and God. When people find a fault on your life, they're going to say, 'That's Youth Pastor Will and Nellie's kids, that's House of Deliverance's youth, that's Apostle's grandchildren.'" When Lil Will and his siblings were growing up, they never liked people calling them the Willises because they felt labeled, but when Lil Will got older, he understood and appreciated who he was.

Lil Will had many people to come into his life and admire him. Many youths wanted to consider Lil Will their friend or brother, but he did not realize that they admired him because of Christ in his life, the maturity, and wisdom. Sometimes, they wanted advice and counsel. Men and women of God said they admired him because he stood for God. One man of God always told Lil Will, "When I grow up, I want to be just like you," even though he was an adult and Lil Will was a young man.

Lil Will's parents always wanted five kids, but they only had four because of complications with Nellie's 4th pregnancy. The gynecologist told Nellie that each pregnancy was getting more difficult and was "taking a toll" on her body. After the fourth child, the gynecologist recommended that they do not have any more kids because they could not promise she or the baby would make it. As years passed by, two big events impacted Will Jr and Nellie's lives in August and September 2005. First, Hurricane Katrina, one of the worst hurricanes in United States history, hit New Orleans, forcing the Willis family to move to Atlanta, Georgia. Lil Will's grandparents and pregnant aunt, Will Jr's sister, went to Jackson, Mississippi. The Willis Family stayed in Atlanta about a week, until Lil Will's father got a phone call that his sister had the baby. This brings us to the second big event, the birth of Lathaniel C. Green Jr. also known as Lil G, which stood for Gentleman and Gift from God. Lil Will's pregnant aunt had to evacuate during the hurricane, knowing that the baby was due soon. Lil Will prayed that the baby would be born on September 2, because that was his birthday. God answered his prayer. Though it was a time of disaster, God brought the family a bundle of joy. It was amazing how things worked out. Lil Will was the first grandchild and Lil G was the last grandchild born on the same day. While in Mississippi, displaced from home, the Willis Family took to baby, Lil G. Lil Will's aunt did not have to worry about anything. Whatever she needed concerning the baby, the Willis family would take care of it. Lil Will's aunt asked his parents to be the godparents of Lil G. Lil Will's parents were very excited because they looked at it as though he was their fifth child that they always wanted. As years went by, Lil G spent much time with the Willis family. There were times when Lil G was not with them and people would ask Lil Will's parents, "Where's your youngest son?" Lil G was always with them, and he even called and introduced Lil Will and his siblings as his big brothers and sisters. When he would get up in church to testify, he used to say, "I thank God for my big brothers and sisters." Even though they were his cousins. They loved him as their little brother.

CHAPTER 4

Ministry/Music

Lil Will was reared in a church that taught and lived the Word of God and promoted the standards of holiness in the spirit of love. The name of the church was House of Deliverance Church, Inc., under the leadership of his great-grandmother, Apostle Mary J. Trask, Overseer. The church members had patterned their lives according to the Word of God and operated under the leading and anointing of the Holy Ghost. Lil Will still attends there today.

Before Lil Will was born, his parents prayed and asked God for children that would serve and work in the ministry for Him. God told his parents, "It is what you put in them that determines their service unto Me."

While Lil Will's mother was pregnant, his father would place his hand on her belly and prophesy what his children would be. As the children grew, their parents would teach them while at home and allow them to lead prayer and read the Word of God and explain it. The parents would question them after church services to see if they were paying attention. Their parents did not put emphasis on balls or dolls, but mics and musical instruments. Their parents knew that if they did not get them involved in the church services then they would get bored. So, they taught the children how to testify and break down the Word of God so that they would be able to participate. The children grew to love church. They never wanted to be late and if for some reason their parents were not able to attend church, the children took it upon themselves to find a ride.

Lil Will's love for music began to grow and his parents noticed how much he admired HOD keyboardist, Minister Samuel Green, who was the HOD praise and worship leader and a gospel recording artist. Lil Will admired him and listened to his music so much that it aggravated his family. They used to ask him to please play something else. Eventually, his parents asked the Man of God (Min. Sam) if he would take Lil Will under his wing and teach him how to play music. The man of God and Lil Will grew close as the years passed, and Lil Will improved on the keyboard. Lil Will looked at Min. Sam as his sensei because he showed and taught him the "ins and outs" of the music industry and ministry. They grew so close that the man of God became his godfather. During church services, Lil Will's parents got permission for him to sit next to the man of God and learn while watching him play. After a while, Lil Will was able to get on the keyboard and play during offering time in order to get some experience. One day, the church keyboardist injured his hand severely at work, which opened the door for Lil Will to begin his music ministry. Just when everything was looking good for Lil Will and his growth in music, Hurricane Katrina hit New Orleans, Louisiana and displaced everyone. Lil Will, his siblings, his parents, and a few other loved ones lived in Jackson, Mississippi and Lafayette, Louisiana for a while. A month before returning home, the city was in a devastating state, but they knew if they could just get the church doors back open all would be blessed. Apostle Mary Trask urged everyone who made it back home to help clean the church. By December, the church was reopened. The church keyboardist was not back home yet, so Lil Will picked back up where he left off. After a year and a half, Min. Sam returned to his position as Minister of Music at House of Deliverance and Lil Will's music teacher, and as Min. Sam began to travel and evangelize, he brought Lil Will with him to play the keyboard and sing with the HOD praise team and other young people.

A couple of ministers prophesied into Lil Will's life because they saw Moses in him. The zealous Lil Will asked his Apostle if he could preach a message. Apostle approved, and at the age of thirteen, Lil Will preached his first message "Fishing for Jesus (Getting a Relationship with Christ)". As Min. Sam grew closer to God, yielded to a Pastoral calling on his life and started his own ministry. God had Min. Sam to teach Lil Will, so one day he could take over. As time went on, Lil Will improved on the keyboard and drew closer to God.

A few years later, while Apostle was giving her final comment during service, Apostle stopped and looked at Lil Will and told him to get ready to preach the gospel and that he would bring forth the Word at the next youth service. That youth service, at the age of fifteen, Lil Will brought forth his message entitled "Let the Fire Flow; Let the Ice Break." That was the beginning of his ministry. Lil Will drew closer to God, and many noticed. They encouraged him and some began to call him a watchman, because God revealed things to him that He did not reveal to others and told him things that would encourage and warn His people. Many adults began to admire the calling in his life as he walked with God.

Just like his godfather, Lil Will started his own teen praise team (New Generation on Fire) and an all-boys group (G3; God's Gifts). Lil Will's father always told him that at the end of the day his siblings were all he would have left. As years went by, friends left the group and church, but family was still there.

While at Beginning Visions Progressive Academy, the youth, who were also members of House of Deliverance, nominated Lil Will to ask the Apostle about them conducting their own service. The plan was to show her what they were able to do at their youth shut-in. Lil Will and the young people began to practice at recess. He gathered the kids together and formed a choir, he led the praise team, and the young people told him he should also do the preaching. So, that night, it was time for the youth shut-in and the kids told Apostle what they would like to do. Apostle smiled and said, "Ok." The young people had a mini-service that night with an MC, testimonies, praise and worship, and Lil Will did a short message.

Lil Will and the young people succeeded in showing Apostle they were able to conduct a service without assistance. Apostle was blessed by what the young people had done but not surprised because she knew they had it in them.

In the beginning of the New Year of 2012, Apostle had an anointing and ordination service. Lil Will was anointed, but not ordained, as a youth minister. As the years went by, Lil Will grew stronger in the Lord and leadership took notice. They gave him more responsibilities and officially promoted him to Minister of Music. He had gone from being one of the youths in the church's youth organization called S.H.Y. (Saved, Holy, and Young) to taking on more responsibilities over the youth and became assistant coordinator of the S.H.Y. Conference, which was a youth revival.

On March 17, 2013, Apostle Mary Trask got heavily afflicted. As the years went by, Apostle progressed slowly. While Apostle was recovering, Pastor Cornelius Trask watched over the congregation.

On Tuesday, July 7, 2018, Lil Will preached a message entitled "The Knowledge of Good and Evil of the Church". Pastor Trask and Assistant Pastor Hawkins were touched so much by the Word that God gave Lil Will, that they asked him to preach it again on the third Sunday for youth service in August. Lil Will brought forth the message, and the Lord anointed his words so much that the second time was more powerful than the first. Two weeks later, on Sunday, September 2, Lil Will's birthday, a minister at House of Deliverance Church preached, ministered into his life, and told him that if he stayed with God, he would be blessed. At the end of the service, Assistant Pastor Hawkins stood up and asked Lil Will to come to the altar. Lil Will came from behind the keyboard, unsure as to why he was being called to the altar. Assistant Pastor told Lil Will, "Pastor and I would like to ordain you as youth minister of House of Deliverance." That birthday was a special day for Lil Will.

CHAPTER 5

Godsons

When Lil Will was a teen, he had a love for kids and kids loved him. So, Lil Will wanted to christen one of the little children in the church. Lil Will saw a young boy, Tyrick Nelson, that caught his attention. What caught Lil Will's eye about Tyrick was they shared similar interests—he liked outdoor activities, loved nature, was fascinated with dirt bikes, liked being a comedian, enjoyed pulling pranks, but most importantly, he loved being a gentleman. He was very curious and got bored quickly; he had to be active. Surprisingly, he was a quietly shy young boy, but if he was close to you, he was more comfortable being himself. Lil Will so much of himself in Tyrick that he was compel to get permission to mentor the little one and asked the young boy's parents. The parents said, "Yes," because they saw God in Lil Will's life and considered him a good role model for their son. Lil Will tried his best to be active with Tyrick. He tried to do right by Tyrick by helping him become the man he wanted to be in life. Everything always did not go as planned, but Lil Will did whatever it took to help him become a little man of God. Lil Will went beyond the call of duty as a godfather. Sometimes people had to let him know that Tyrick was not his son. Lil Will was being more like a surrogate father. Many people were shocked and inspired because of how young he was taking on the responsibility of a godfather. Some said, "We need young men like that. I wish my son was like you." Lil Will started a routine with his godson by praying and reading and explaining the Word every day. Lil Will also gave him words of wisdom and inspiration, such as, "You are a man of God, gentleman, and soldier." Also, he reminded him of the three r's, which are be Real, Righteous, and Respectful. That was the spiritual side, but on the natural side, being guys, they were very competitive. They also challenged and pranked each other. They made fun deals and bets; and they talked for hours about the things they loved, such as music and animals.

As Tyrick got older it was not just a godson-godfather relationship but a friend-brother relationship like Alfred and Bruce Wayne, Batman and Robin, David and Jonathan, Jermaine Dupri and Shad Moss, Will Smith and Phil (father-and-son relationship), Will Smith and Carlton (brother relationship), and Will Smith and Jazz (friend relationship). The crazy thing was the fact that Will and Tyrick were seven years apart. Lil Will realized that being a good godfather called for him to step into many roles. Throughout their relationship, Lil Will had sometimes been like a big brother, sometimes a friend, and sometimes a godfather. Their relationship birthed the BFF company. It took much praying, fasting, counseling, spending time together, and finding things for Tyrick to do to make sure he stayed out of trouble (like working for money). Lil Will made sure that Tyrick got a balance of spiritual and natural values. In his teen years, Tyrick told Lil Will that he thanked God for him because he didn't know where he would be if it were not for him; he could be in jail or dead.

When Tyrick was younger, Lil Will promised him that he would be the only godson. Years later, Tyrick's uncle and family, the Burris family, joined House of Deliverance Church. They noticed how Will interacted with Tyrick. Lil Will noticed and took interest in their little toddler, Tyrone, and wanted to christen him as well. One day, Lil Will and the Burris family discussed the christening of Tyrone, but Lil Will remembered the promise he made to Tyrick. One Sunday, Lil Will and Tyrick were getting the sound system ready for service and Tyrick said, "*Parrain*, I know you promised me that I would be your only godchild, but I wanted to know if I can have a godbrother?" Lil Will looked at Tyrick with the feeling of curiosity and said, "Tell me who it is." Tyrick said, "Tyrone." Lil Will smiled and said, "Yes." And the rest was history. Tyrone McGhee was an active young man, friendly, a gentleman who loved helping others, a gamer, and an outdoors person. He was fascinated with first responders, especially K-9 police.

Throughout Tyrick's childhood and teen life, Lil Will was being a mentor to other young men, and he loved and enjoyed being a mentor and trying to find ways to keep them busy. Lil Will worked at a summer camp for young men as a mentor and a role model. He also worked as a lead teacher at an elementary college preparatory charter school.

A PECULIAR YOUNG MAN

Lil Will had a Yamaha Mo 8 keyboard and music production software, Steinberg Cubase Le 4

Lil Will's first car, Honda Accord 2004

One of Lil Will's greatest professors, Dr. Stephen Andrus Sr., at Delgado Community College. Words that Dr. Andrus said that hold to Lil Will's heart was "Never say Never." That might be a cliché to everyone. But when Lil Will heard his life story, he understood why Mr. Andrus utilized the phrase.

Lil Will and his siblings are at their auntie's house for Christmas.

Lil Will at Delgado Community College around phenomenal African American executive dean females with PhD.

Lil Will played the organ learning from his godfather, music teacher, and role model, Pastor Samuel Green.

Many people called and knew her "The Powerful Woman of God, Who Won't Take Down!"

A PECULIAR YOUNG MAN

Lil Will and his sister's first year worked at Élan Academy Charter School under the leadership of Dr. Melanie Askew-Clark.

Lil Will at a Recording Studio

Lil Will, siblings, and parents dog. Lil Will and his siblings were so excited when they found out they were going to have a puppy. Miss Midnight (M-n-M)

Lil Will and his siblings completed their GED. But that didn't stop him from continuing his education.

A PECULIAR YOUNG MAN

One of Lil Will's favorite pictures. He was 12 years old at his church school banquet.

WILL WILLIS III

Lil Will was on the keyboard, his brother was on the drums, and his sister was singing a solo.

A PECULIAR YOUNG MAN

Lil Will played at a Recital.

Lil Will and his Godsons. Lil Will was a teenager, being a mentor to them.

Lil Will and his family. Lil Will's cousin, Lathaniel Green, was always with them.

A PECULIAR YOUNG MAN

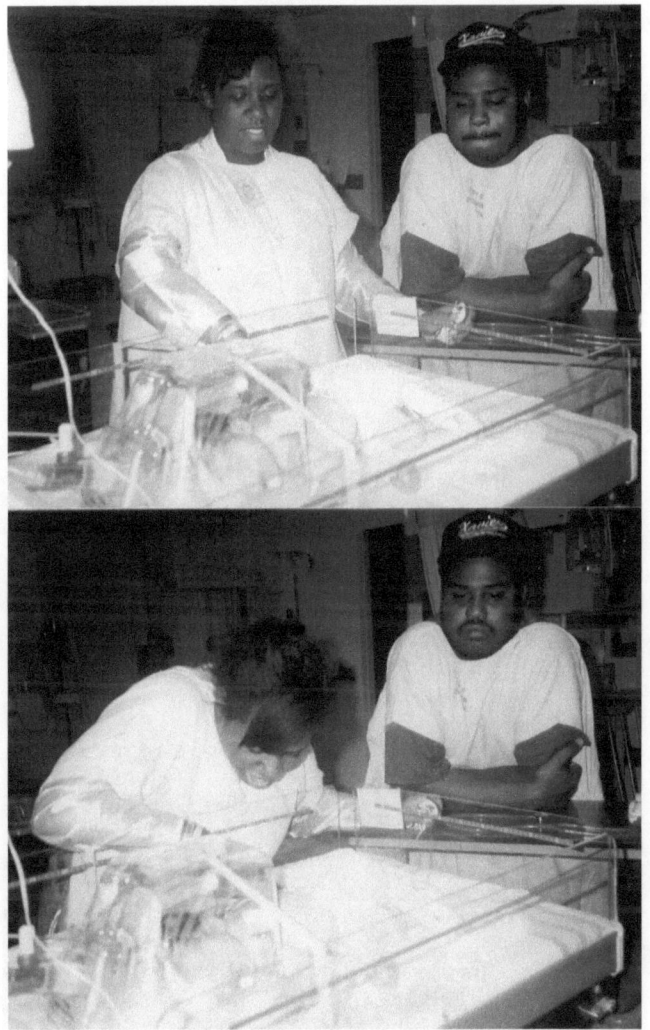

This is Lil Will's parents watching Lil Will in an incubator. Hoping and praying for God's miracle.

Lil Will's kindergarten graduation picture.

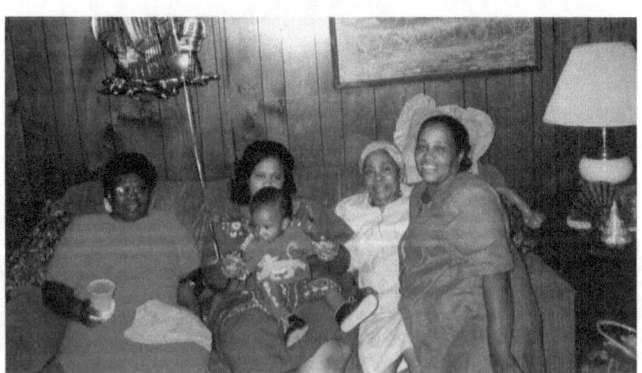

Lil Will's Grandmothers and Great Grandmothers. Holiness was their life. From Left to Right: Apostle Mary J. Trask, Elder Viola T. Spencer, Sr. Ellena Martin Jones, Evangelist Annette Jones Bickham. Can you guess who didn't like taking pictures?

A PECULIAR YOUNG MAN

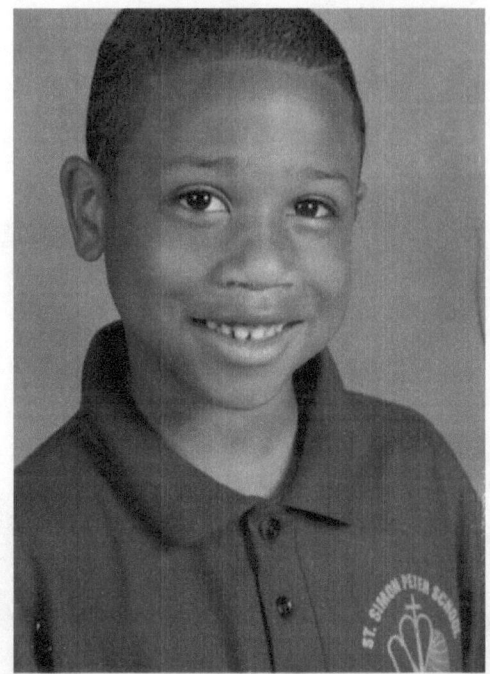

Lil Will in Kindergarten or First Grade at St. Simon Peter.

Yep! That's Lil Will!

Lil Will and his siblings got medals at the ACE Regional Student Convention. Their school had plaques for second place in Platform and first place in Music.

Lil Will and siblings have sung "The Star Spangled Banner" at the graduation.

A PECULIAR YOUNG MAN

CHAPTER 6

Overcoming Flaws

Lil Will was never a person who would get into or start trouble. He did not want to disappoint God, his church, or his family, but just like any other young person, he made some mistakes in his life. This chapter will show how Lil Will overcame some of the flaws and mistakes that kept him from progressing in his walk with God. Most people may not think that these flaws were a big deal, but to Lil Will and God they were significant.

From a young age, Lil Will fought with the spirit of fear. Fear came to him at night in his sleep, especially if there was a death in the family. Lil Will tried leaving the television on, but when certain movies or sounds came on, it would cause him to have nightmares. There were nights when he would climb into bed with his parents. His father told him that he also had problems with fear as a young man, and his mother told him to pray and sleep with his Bible and fear could not touch him if he believed. So, Lil Will tried it. Instead of leaving his television on any channel, he put it on a gospel station and slept with his Bible. Now when fear visited, Lil Will had something to fight with.

Lil Will also struggled with anger. The Bible says, "Be angry and sin not," (Epesians 4:26) but there were many times Lil Will wanted to react. He wanted to get back at the person who wronged him. He got out of character with them, but afterward he felt bad because he allowed the devil to bring him to that place. He had to continue to remind himself that the Bible says, "Vengeance is mine said the Lord." (Romans 12:19 KJV)

Lil Will had a problem with giving, not just to people, but to God. Lil Will did not like letting go of his money. He was afraid that if he gave, he would not get it back. He would pay his tithes (10%) to the Lord, but that was it. He did not try to give any other type of offering. Lil Will felt that he gave what was required of him to give. He used to hear testimonies of people giving and being blessed by giving, and it made him sad. He was sad because he wanted to feel what they felt, but the thought of giving up his money and not knowing if he would get it back bothered him. Lil Will liked to see his money, as he says, "stacking," and did not like his stack to be low. Lil Will felt like he had other responsibilities to take care of for himself. If he had something left over, he would take care of God. He did not put God first. If his family would ask for money, most times he would say that he did not have it. If he decided to contribute or help with something, he did not do it with a smile on his face. Through counseling from leadership and much prayer, Lil Will became a giver to the Lord, the church, and others in need. Now, do not get it twisted. He still saves his money, but he realizes that it feels good to bless others. He believes when he gives to the Lord or helps others, God blesses him in many ways.

The Bible says that beauty is vain, and the spirit of vanity was upon Lil Will as a youngster. There is nothing wrong with looking nice, but when you do it for the reason of having people desire you or lust after you, then you are sinning. Lil Will said that he looked nice only to get the young ladies at church and school to like him. He looked good and he knew it, and if another young man came to the church or school and took some of the attention from him, he would get upset and jealous. Lil Will soon realized this was not the spirit of God, and he did not like the way it made him feel. Lil Will's desire was to be more and more like Jesus. He realized that Jesus did not focus on self, but he was focused Kingdom work for God. Through prayer and seeking God, Lil Will was freed from the spirit of vanity.

Another flaw of Lil Will was impatience. Many people have impatient moments, but Lil Will was always impatient. Over the years, he got better through prayer, but he still has to check himself from time to time.

No, Lil Will did not do drugs, drink alcohol, or commit fornicate, but his main addiction was masturbation. Many people said that it was not a sin, but the Bible says in Hebrews 12:1 KJV "…let us lay aside every weight and the sin which doth so easily beset us," and I John 2:16 states "For all that is in the world, the lust of the flesh, and the lust of the eyes, and the pride of life, is not of the Father, but is of the world." Masturbation was a weight, and it had become a sin in Lil Will's life. Lil Will was a little boy and was bound to it. One day at the age of nine Lil Will was in pain from masturbating and it frightened him. So, he went to his father. As his father was talking to him, he did not know what he was doing had a name and that other people did it also. His father told him that he was once addicted to masturbating and it was not of God. His father told him that he needed to pray and ask God to help him before it turned to lust. Lil Will's father thanked him for coming to him and told him that if he ever had a problem to make sure he always found someone in spiritual authority to talk to. Lil Will grew in the Lord, and he wanted to stop this addiction. He remembered that his father told him to ask for help, but he was ashamed and afraid of what others would think. Lil Will tried to overcome the addiction on his own, but over and over again, he found himself doing it and telling the Lord, "I'm sorry, Lord. This is my last time." Then one day, the enemy came and tried to tempt him again and Lil Will said, "No, I am not going to do it: I am tired of being defeated and disappointing Jesus." It was a struggle because the feeling did not want to leave, but Lil Will remembered that the Bible says, "…resist the enemy and he must flee." The enemy lost that night and Lil Will felt good. Lil Will realized that it could have been easier if he would have called someone and asked them to pray with him against the enemy. One chases a thousand, but two chase ten thousand demons.

The Bible says, "…thinketh no evil…" and it also says, "Let this mind be in you, which was in Christ Jesus." This chapter has a lot to do with the mind, and Lil Will learned that just because you do not actually do what you think about, it does not mean you are not sinning. To think about doing something that Jesus would not do is sin. It does not matter how small it is. If a thought that wasn't Christ-like came to Lil Will's mind, he simply began to do what Christ did, resist the devil. The Bible says, "Resist the Devil, and he shall flee.

CHAPTER 8

Epilogue

Lil Will's goal is to be successful, wealthy, and healthy in God. He wants to be whatever God wants him to be. He has desires and plans in his heart that he would love to do if it is God's will. He has reached a point in his life where he realizes his life is not about him, but it is all about Jesus. He wants to please God and not man. His desire is to remain humble before the Lord. He is all about being wise, having a positive spiritual life, and being addicted to God.

Lil Will is growing in the wisdom, knowledge, and understanding of God and ministry. He is growing in education and knowledge. He is also growing in the knowledge and the skill of business. Lil Will is already becoming more successful in God and maintaining a healthy relationship with Him.

Psalm

Lord, I thank you for the things that you've done, and what you are going to do; and what you already did in my life.

Lord I just don't thank you for what you've done but who you are in my life. Selah.

I just want to repent for all the things I have done wrong.

Cleanse me, wash me purge me.

Lord, deliver me from anything that's not like you. That is not according to your will and your way.

We bind up Every sin, every iniquity, every debt, every transgressions, every evil demonic carnal satanic wicked worldly spirit mind forces imaginations ways.

We bind up lust, flesh, pride, deceitful and lying spirit.

We cast it down from the root where it came from.

Lord teach and give us your ways, commandments, your laws, your precepts, your statutes, your judgments, your will.

Lord reign down your blessing, your healing, your deliverance, your salvation, your working miracle power.

Lord save families, church families, government, friends, associates

Lord, you are the Supreme Being, Creator of the universe.

We say Hallelujah to your name which is one word in every language.

We say Hallelujah to your name which is the Highest Praise. Selah.

All the Heavens, and the earth, and under the earth and the waters shall praise you, magnify you, and worship you. Amen!

Goals; Prayers; Revelations; Proverbs and Sayings; Fun Facts

(G) – Lil Will's Sayings to his Godson's

1. I want the F.L.O.W. to flow in me.

    Faith – is the substance (key)

    Love – is the greatest commandment

    Obedience – is the first commandment with promise

    Wisdom – is the principal thing

2. God means First - #1

    When you have something or someone before God in your life, you've made Him lower than what He should be. Nothing is higher than God in this world, so nothing should be higher than God in your life

3. When you are not saved, there are blessings, but at the end are curses; but when you are saved there will be trials, but at the end will be blessings.

4. You do not need to look for an identity when God has already given you the best one you could have.

5. We are not on Earth to please people, but to help people
6. A real man does not easily give in to vices
7. A gift or skill does not automatically make you a leader
8. Because you're old or have many experiences, that does not mean you are wise
9. A Fact is what I can see; Faith is the Facts I can't see; If you do not have Faith, then you have Fear
10. Servants serve, but masters are greater servants
11. Faith is a gift and a fruit (character)
12. We tend to rely on resources (medicine; man; tech; things; etc.) instead of the source (Jesus Christ)
13. The absence from Jesus Christ (source) is a spiritual famine
14. Being a church member does not mean you are saved
15. I would rather be green then yellow*
16. Why gamble with your life? (Obedience is better than sacrifice)
17. When God uses someone, it does not mean that they are saved…He can use ANY vessel to get his point across
18. Many want a Pentecostal movement, but not a Holiness lifestyle
19. The Devil has a PhD in the Kingdom of Heaven

20. Most of the choices people make in life are influenced by their environment, atmosphere, and/or rearing
21. The three most debatable topics…
    a. Religion
    b. Politics
    c. Culture
22. Most people want to be blessed, but not delivered
23. Be real; Be respectful; Be righteous
24. You are a Man of God; Gentleman; Soldier
25. When you see wrong…
    a. Correct it
    b. Run from it
    c. Tell it
26. We need Three aspects of Life
    a. Prayer Life
    b. Holy Life
    c. Worship Life
27. You should not make fun of anyone especially when you do not know if they are
    a. Disabled
    b. God's people
    c. Angels
28. It is possible to live right without living righteously
29. What may be good may not be righteous

30. Fishing for Jesus: Getting a closer relationship with Him
31. Do not let anything define you but God
32. Having information but no revelation is boredom
33. Is your relationship with Christ personal or just business
34. God did not just call us from sin, but also the pleasures of this world (distraction/weight)
35. Backsliding – leaving from what you have been taught
36. You may know more than your master, but you are never greater than your master
37. Fear – caution; respect
38. God is the same today, yesterday, and forevermore, but he upgrades*
39. Do not despise Fundamental basics (foundation) – Build upon it
40. God wants us clean from the inside out*
41. There is a difference when you believe Him (Christ) and when you believe in Him (Christ)*
42. You can be perfect/Holy, without sin*
43. Because someone is gifted and anointed it does not mean they're living saved
44. If you are praying to God and nothing happens, you must check to see . . .

    a. Are you in the will?
    b. Are you doing something wrong?
    c. Does He see that for your life?
    Nothing is wrong with God; something is wrong with you
45. My prayer is . . . I do not want them to just be saved on earth, but get to place in God so that they make it in the Kingdom of Heaven
46. You do not have to be famous and rich to be successful
47. You do not have to be famous to be rich (vice versa)
48. You may not sin physically, but do you sin mentally?
49. It is not about your age, but finishing and completing what you've started (no matter how long it takes)
50. Three things Lil Will do not like
    a. Dishonesty
    b. Lack of communication
    c. Procrastination
51. Fire does not put out fire, but water does *
52. The crowd is not always right
53. If you say that you do not feel peace, love, or joy and you say you are saved, check your salvation
54. Everyone is a leader and follower
55. God is like numbers, He does not lie

56. The Church is everything you need it to be (Educational; Correctional; Medical; Legal etc.)
57. When you do something wrong, you don't just make yourself look bad, but your family, church, and God (F)
58. Jesus was 100% God and 100% man, but we are 100% man striving to be 100% like God
59. People say, "Don't judge a book by its cover," but I say, "change the cover"
60. Don't let my words be words only
61. Let the Word back up my words
62. You can be forgiven and still receive consequences.
63. It is not about glory, fame, hype, trend, or self, but support, humility, quality.
64. Groom Yourself, don't Change Yourself.
65. God made you who you are for a reason; don't become anything other than what God intended
66. Just because a person is Knowledgeable, that does not mean they are always right
67. Just because you have a responsibility, that does not mean you love or enjoy the responsibility
68. Will had a Samuel experience when he was around his primary school age. He heard the voice of the Lord twice but didn't answer the call because he

was frightened. The voice sounded like his father, but his father was at work

69. Lil Will's brother christened Tyrick's youngest brother.
70. All of Tyrone' siblings were christened by someone in Lil Will's immediate household.

These are just a few of the many revelations Lil Will has had.

Will's Praise Vamp

Will Willis III

Musical Piece

This music came about when the drummer and I went to church playing shouting music. We switched the sound, then the rest was history. We played it at church, and people praised God. It was so high with praise that the Leader of the church said, "The angels are standing."

When to use this piece?

We use this musical piece, some may call it Congregational, call and response, shouting songs, praise, COGIC, traditional, or hymn songs at the vamp of the song. We can wait until the chorus/refrain/verse songs are complete and then do it at the vamp of the song. We do these songs usually between the tempos of 80 and 140. It depends on the speed of your church, your singers, and/or musicians playing and/or singing the song. This musical piece can be done when the singers and musicians start vamping the songs when the bass line hits eight notes. You can change from that regular eight notes to this medley. You can also wait until the singers finish the vamp and then let the music play shouting music when the bass is walking the eight notes, and then come with this piece. If you just playing church praise music, then you can make the change. Do how you feel.

BUSINESS INFORMATION

House of Deliverance Church, Inc
Apostle Mary J. Trask, Overseer
732 Opelousas St.
New Orleans, La 70114
(504)362-6286
ministryinfo@houseofdeliverancechurch.com

Gabrielle Willis
Gabrielle's Cupcake and Paint
@gabriellescupcakeandpaint

Emanuell Willis
Manny Seafood and Soul
@mannyseafoodandsoul

Will Willis III
BFF Corp
Non-profit Organization

www.ingramcontent.com/pod-product-compliance
Lightning Source LLC
LaVergne TN
LVHW092057060526
838201LV00047B/1434